Voice

C000103157

Arranged & Edited by Barrie Carson Turner

Best of Canons and Rounds

From the 13th century to the present day

ED 13170

ISMN M-2201-2746-5
ISBN 978-1-84761-116-1

www.schott-music.com

 SCHOTT

Mainz · London · Madrid · New York · Paris · Prague · Tokyo · Toronto
© 2008 SCHOTT MUSIC Ltd, London • Printed in Germany

ED 13170

British Library Cataloguing-in-Publication Data.
A catalogue record for this book is available from the British Library
ISMN M-2201-2746-5
ISBN 978-1-84761-116-1

Design and cover illustration by www.adamhaystudio.com
Music setting by Enigma Music Production Services
Printed in Germany S&Co.8411

Contents

Editor's note: These canons and rounds can be sung by any number or combination of voices. Parts and ostinatos can be omitted and the melodies may be sung at any pitch.

1. Come, Let Us All (3 parts)

John Hilton (1599–1657)

1. Come, let us all a— may - ing go, and

2. The bells shall ring,— the— bells— shall ring. And the

3. drums shall beat, the fife shall play, and

light - ly, and light - ly trip it to and— fro.

cuck-oo, the cuck-oo, the cuck-oo sing. The

so we'll— spend our— time a - way.

© 2008 Schott Music Ltd, London

2. Sing Together (3 parts)

Traditional

1 Sing, sing to-geth - er, mer-ri-ly, mer-ri-ly sing.

2 Sing, sing to-geth - er, mer-ri-ly, mer-ri-ly sing.

3 Sing, sing, sing, sing.

Ostinato Sing,——— let's sing.———

3. Oh, How Beautiful (4 parts)

Melody: Moritz Hauptmann (1792–1868)
Words: BCT

1. **2.** Oh, how beau - ti - ful the

3. **4.** sound of church bells ring - ing.

4. Were I a Little Bird (3 parts)

Clara Schumann (1819–1896)
Words adapted BCT

1 — Were I a lit - tle bird,

2 — and had two ti - ny wings,

3 — I would fly home to you.

Ostinato — I would fly home.

5. The Flowers on the Hillside (2 parts)

Melody: Traditional
Words: BCT

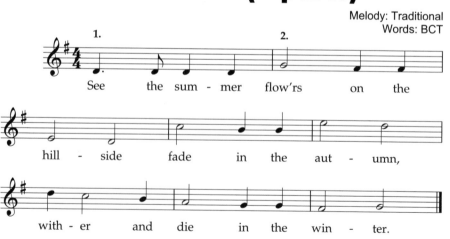

See the sum - mer flow'rs on the

hill - side fade in the aut - umn,

with - er and die in the win - ter.

6. Sanctus (4 parts)

Anon.

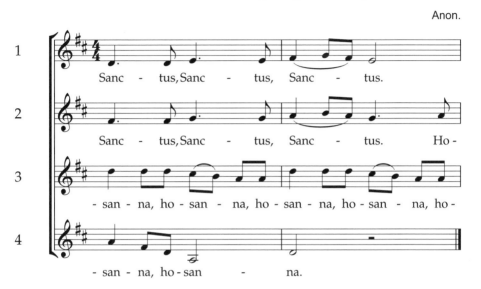

7. Jubilate Deo (6 parts)

Michael Praetorius (1571–1621)

8. Come, Honest Friends (3 parts)

Simon Ives (1600–1662)

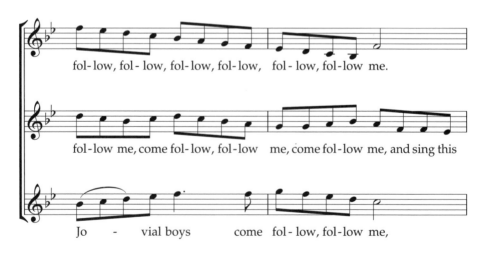

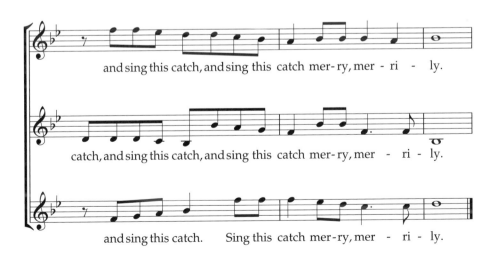

9. Let Us Hurry On (4 parts)

Traditional

10. Oliver Cromwell (2 parts)

Traditional
Arranged BCT

1.

O - li - ver Crom-well lay bu - ried and dead,
ap - ples were ripe and quite rea - dy to fall,
sad - dle and bri - dle they lie on the shelf,

2.

hee - haw, bu - ried and dead. There
hee - haw, rea - dy to fall. There
hee - haw, lie on the shelf. And

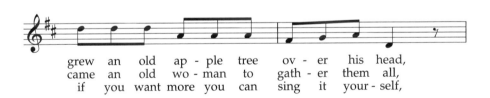

grew an old ap - ple tree ov - er his head,
came an old wo - man to gath - er them all,
if you want more you can sing it your - self,

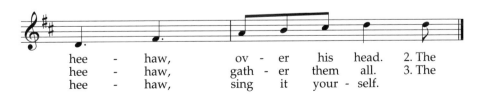

hee - haw, ov - er his head. 2. The
hee - haw, gath - er them all. 3. The
hee - haw, sing it your - self.

11. By the Waters
of Babylon (3 parts)

Traditional

By———————— the wa - ters, the

wa - - ters of Ba - by - lon

we sat down and wept,——— and

wept,——— for thee, Zi - on.

We re - mem - ber thee, re - mem - ber

thee, re - mem - ber thee, Zi - on.

12. Three Merry Boys (3 parts)

William Lawes (1602–1645)

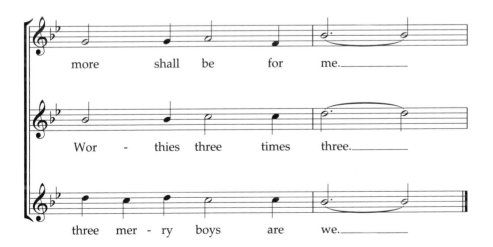

The Wise Men were but seven, ne'er

The mu - ses were but nine, the

And three mer - ry boys, and three mer - ry boys, and

more shall be for me.

Wor - thies three times three.

three mer - ry boys are we.

13. The Bells of Oseney (3 parts)

Anon. (17th c.)

1 — The great bells of Ose - ney,

2 — they ring, they jing, they ring, they jing.

3 — The ten - or go - eth mer - ri - ly.

14. Dip, Dip and Swing (2 parts)

Margaret Embers McGee

My pad - dle's keen and bright, flash-ing with sil - ver.

Fol - low the wild goose flight, dip, dip and swing.

Ostinato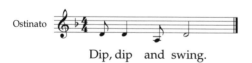

Dip, dip and swing.

15. Sing Out, Sing Loud (3 parts)

Melody: Traditional
Words: BCT

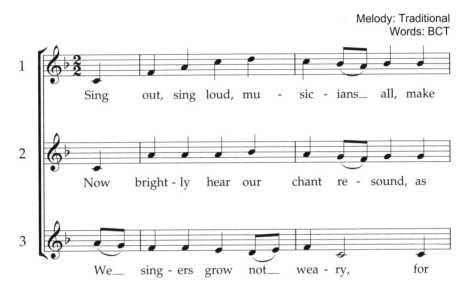

16. Hey Down Derry (3 parts)

John Hilton (1599–1657)

17. Row the Boat, Whittington (3 parts)

Anon. (17th or 18th c.)

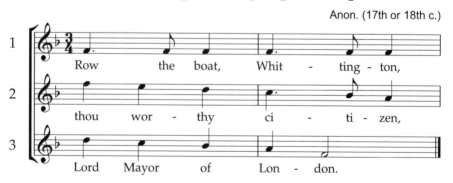

18. Tallis's Canon (4 parts)

Thomas Tallis (c.1505–1585)

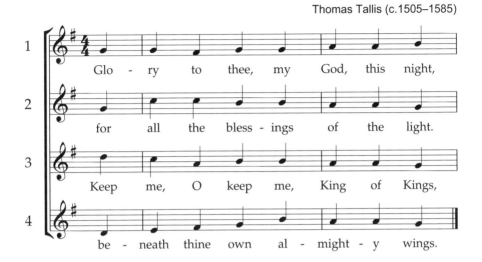

1. Glo - ry to thee, my God, this night,
2. for all the bless - ings of the light.
3. Keep me, O keep me, King of Kings,
4. be - neath thine own al - might - y wings.

19. Time to Wake (2 parts)

Melody: Johann Jakob Wachsmann (1791–1853)
Words adapted BCT

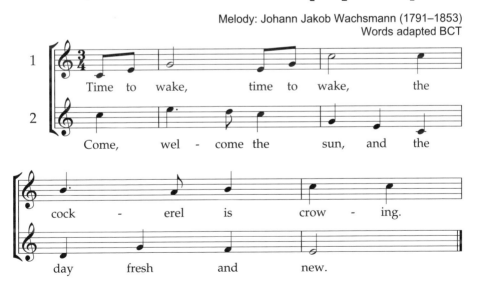

Time to wake, time to wake, the
Come, wel - come the sun, and the

cock - erel is crow - ing.
day fresh and new.

20. Oh, How Lovely is the Evening (3 parts)

Traditional

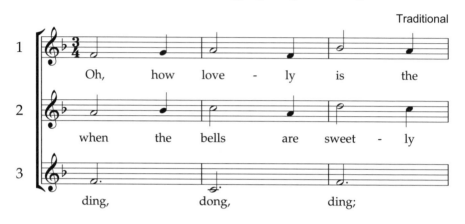

Oh, how love - ly is the
when the bells are sweet - ly
ding, dong, ding;

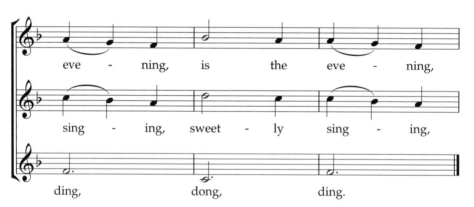

eve - ning, is the eve - ning,
sing - ing, sweet - ly sing - ing,
ding, dong, ding.

21. Ars longa (4 parts)

Ludwig van Beethoven (1770–1827)

Ars lon - ga, vi - ta bre - vis.

22. Morgenstund hat Gold im Mund (3 parts)

Friedrich Silcher (1789–1860)

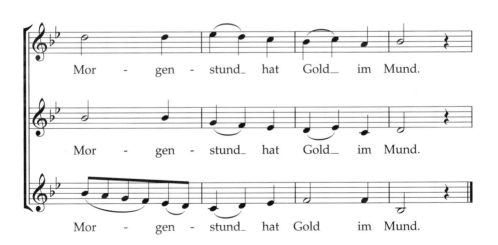

Translation: The early bird catches the worm.

23. Heaven and Earth (3 parts)

Anon.
Melody & Words adapted BCT

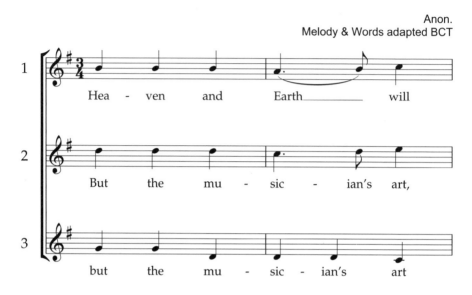

1. Hea - ven and Earth____ will

2. But the mu - sic - ian's art,

3. but the mu - sic - ian's art

both fade a - way.

but the mu - sic - ian's art,

ev - er will stay.

24. Great Tom is Cast (3 parts)

William Lawes (1602–1645)

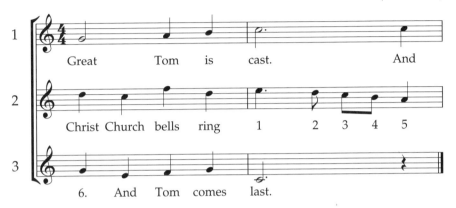

25. If You Trust Before You Try (3 parts)

Charles Frederick Lampe (?1739–?1769)

26. I Am a Poor Man (3 parts)

Traditional
Words adapted BCT

27. Christmastime is Here (2 parts)

Barrie Carson Turner

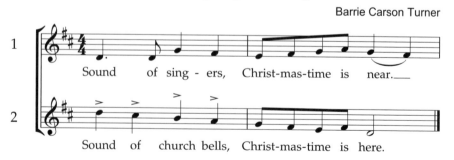

28. Birthday Round (4 parts)

Traditional
Adapted BCT

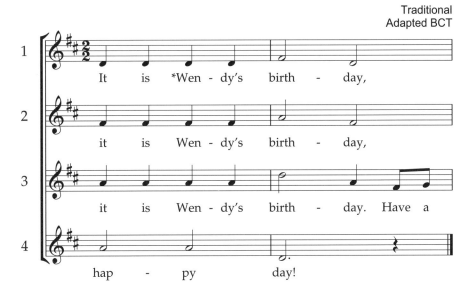

*Name as appropriate

29. The Higher the Plum Tree (4 parts)

William Lawes (1602–1645)

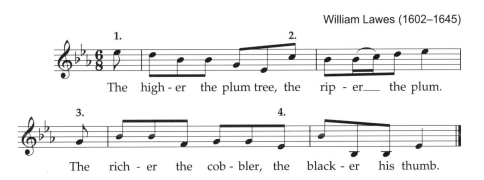

30. Come, Follow Me (3 parts)

John Hilton (1599–1657)

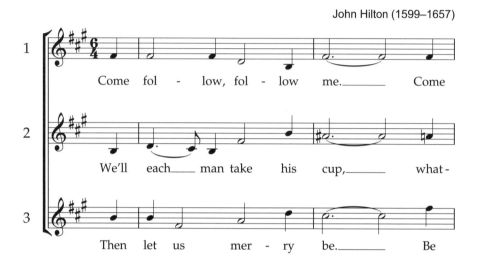

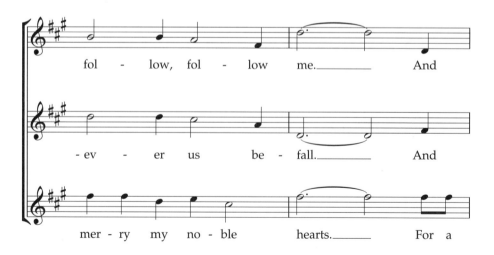

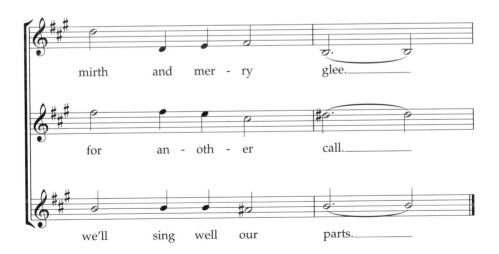

31. Shalom chaverim (3 parts)

Israeli Traditional

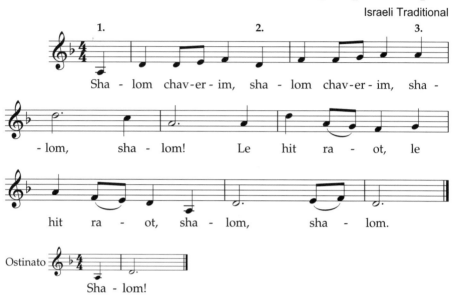

Sha - lom chav-er - im, sha - lom chav-er - im, sha -
- lom, sha - lom! Le hit ra - ot, le
hit ra - ot, sha - lom, sha - lom.

Ostinato

Sha - lom!

Translation: Peace friends, until we meet again.

32. The USH Round (3 parts)

Barrie Carson Turner

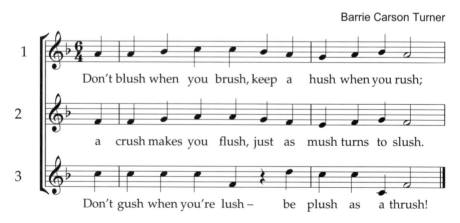

Don't blush when you brush, keep a hush when you rush;

a crush makes you flush, just as mush turns to slush.

Don't gush when you're lush – be plush as a thrush!

33. Dona nobis pacem (3 parts)

Anon.

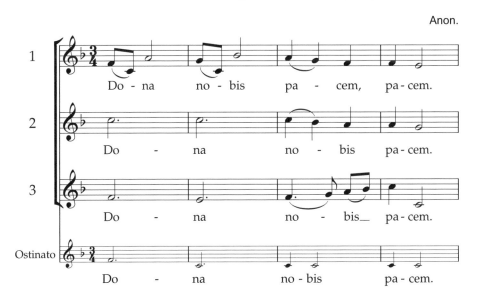

34. Viva la musica (4 parts)

Anon.

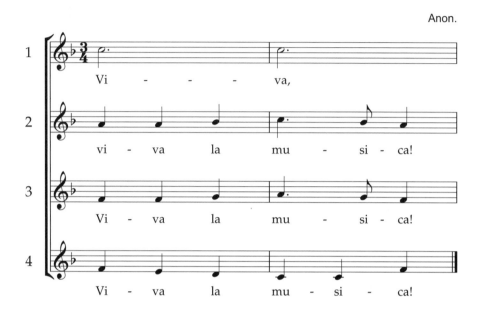

35. Join and Sing (4 parts)

Melody: Carl Gottlieb Hering (1766–1853)
Words: BCT

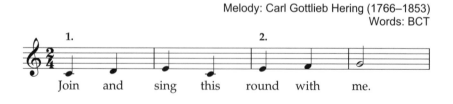

36. Long Live Our King (3 parts)

Anon. (17th or 18th c.)

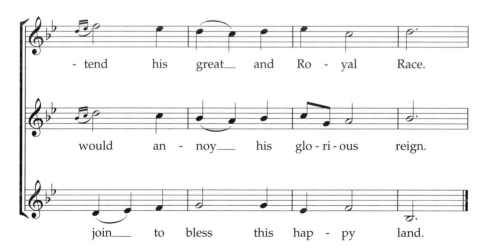

1 Long live our King__ and may all grace at -

2 May all their ef - forts prove in vain who

3 Then peace and plen - ty, hand__ in hand, shall

- tend his great__ and Ro - yal Race.

would an - noy__ his glo - ri - ous reign.

join__ to bless this hap - py land.

© 2008 Schott Music Ltd, London

37. An Old Epitaph (3 parts)

Henry Purcell (1659–1695)

38. Hullabaloo-Balay (2 parts)

Traditional
Arranged BCT

Me fa - ther kept a board - ing house,

hul - la - ba - loo - ba - lay,_____

hul - la - ba - loo - ba - lay - ba - lay. The

board - ing house was on the quay,

hul - la - ba - loo - ba - lay._____

Ostinato

Hul - la - ba - loo - ba - lay - ba - lay.

39. Rock-a My Soul (3 parts)

Traditional
Adapted BCT

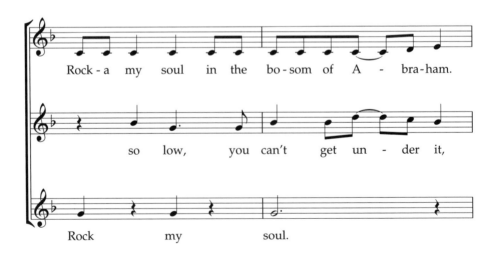

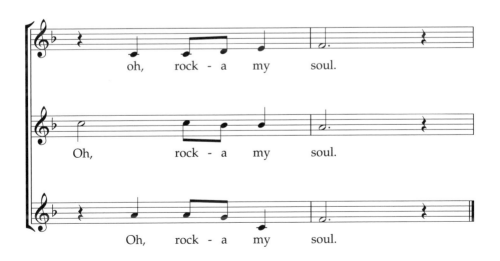

40. When Ever I Marry (3 parts)

John Hilton (1599–1657)

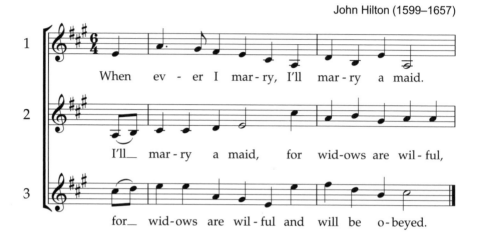

41. Bless Them That Curse You (3 parts)

John Hilton (1599–1657)

42. Nach der Arbeit ist gut ruh'n (3 parts)

Friedrich Silcher (1789–1860)

1
Nach der Ar - beit ist gut ruh'n,

2
Nach der Ar - beit ist gut ruh'n,

3
Nach der Ar - beit ist gut ruh'n,

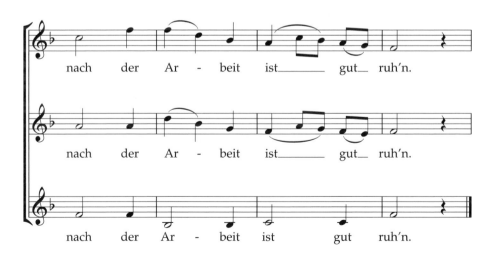

nach der Ar - beit ist gut ruh'n.

nach der Ar - beit ist gut ruh'n.

nach der Ar - beit ist gut ruh'n.

Translation: You can't beat a good old sit down after a hard slog.

43. Célébrons sans cesse (4 parts)

Orlando di Lasso (1532–1594)

Translation: Celebrate, without ceasing, the gifts of God.

44. Ah, Poor Bird (4 parts)

Anon. (18th c.)

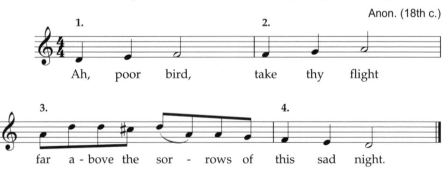

45. Winter is Over (4 parts)

Melody: Traditional
Words: BCT

46. Zum, Gali, Gali (4 parts)

Traditional
Adapted BCT

47. Flow'rs are Dying (4 parts)

Traditional

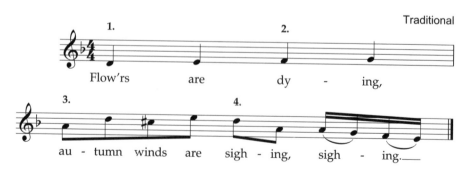

48. The Silver Swan (3 parts)

John Smith (1712–1795)

49. The Post! (4 parts)

Melody: Traditional
Words: BCT

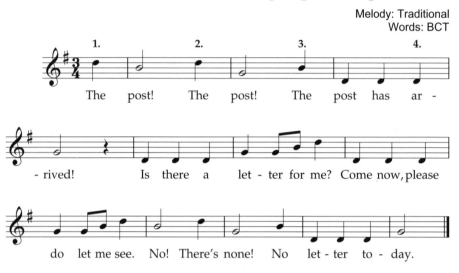

The post! The post! The post has ar -

- rived! Is there a let - ter for me? Come now, please

do let me see. No! There's none! No let - ter to - day.

50. Cherries So Ripe (4 parts)

Old street cry

Cher - ries so ripe and so round, the best in the

mar - ket___ found, on - ly a pen - ny a

pound. Who_____ will buy?

51. A Chiding Catch (3 parts)

Henry Purcell (1659–1695)

52. Viva la musica (3 parts)

Michael Praetorius (1571–1621)

53. I Like the Flowers (3 parts)

Melody: Traditional
Words adapted BCT

54. The Hills are Resounding (3 parts)

Melody: Traditional
Words: BCT

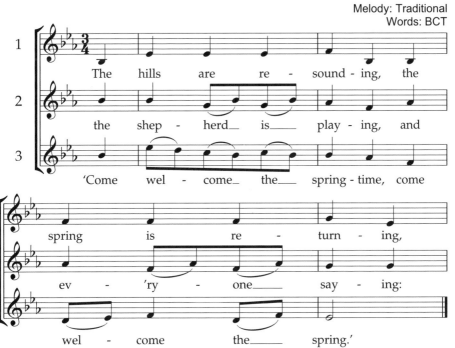

1. The hills are re - sound - ing, the spring is re - turn - ing,
2. the shep - herd is play - ing, and ev - 'ry - one say - ing:
3. 'Come wel - come the spring - time, come wel - come the spring.'

55. Worship and Praise (3 parts)

Melody: Traditional
Words adapted BCT

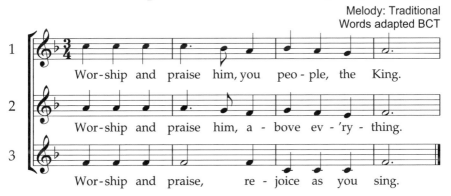

1. Wor-ship and praise him, you peo - ple, the King.
2. Wor-ship and praise him, a - bove ev - 'ry - thing.
3. Wor-ship and praise, re - joice as you sing.

© 2008 Schott Music Ltd, London

56. Follow Me (3 parts)

Edmund Nelham (17th c.)

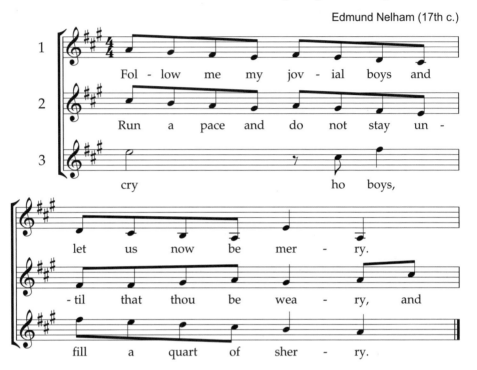

57. All in to Service (3 parts)

Henry Purcell (1659–1695)

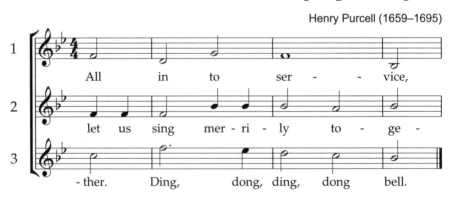

58. The Truth Falters Never (3 parts)

Friedrich Schneider (1786–1853)
Words adapted BCT

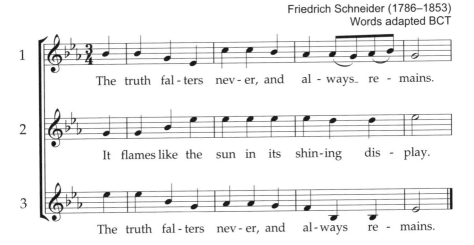

1. The truth fal-ters nev-er, and al-ways_ re - mains.

2. It flames like the sun in its shin-ing dis - play.

3. The truth fal-ters nev-er, and al-ways re - mains.

59. Wintertime is Drawing Closer (3 parts)

Barrie Carson Turner

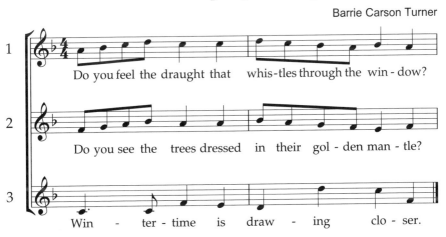

1. Do you feel the draught that whis-tles through the win - dow?

2. Do you see the trees dressed in their gol - den man - tle?

3. Win - ter-time is draw - ing clo - ser.

60. Come, Follow Me (3 parts)

John Hilton (1599–1657)

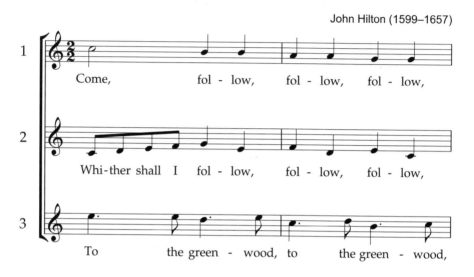

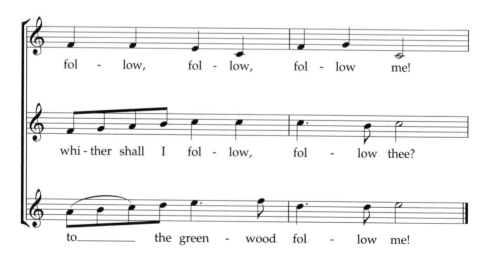

61. Chairs to Mend (3 parts)

N. American Traditional

Chairs to mend, old chairs to mend!

Rush or cane bot - tom, old chairs to mend, old

chairs to mend. New__ mack - er - el, new

mack - er - el! New mack - er - el, new

mack - er - el! Old rags, an - y

old rags? Take mo - ney for your old

rags. An - y hare skins or rab - bit skins?

50

62. Everybody Loves
Saturday Night (2 parts)

Traditional Nigerian
Arranged BCT

Ev - 'ry - bo - dy loves Sat - ur-day night.

Ev - 'ry - bo - dy loves Sat - ur-day

night. Ev - 'ry-bo - dy, ev - 'ry-bo - dy,

ev - 'ry-bo - dy, ev - 'ry-bo - dy, ev - 'ry - bo - dy

loves Sat - ur-day night. They love Sat - ur-day.

Ostinato

Ev - 'ry - bo - dy loves Sat - ur day.

63. Rose, Rose (4 parts)

Traditional
Arranged BCT

1 Rose, rose, rose, rose,

2 shall I ev - er see thee wed?

3 I shall mar - ry at thy will,

4 at thy___ will._____

Double
ostinato

Rose, rose, rose.

Rose, rose, rose.

Note: The ostinato singers should stand either side of the choir.

64. My Dame Had a Lame Tame Crane (4 parts)

Anon. (17th c.)

65. Sing and Rejoice (4 parts)

William Bradbury (1816–1868)

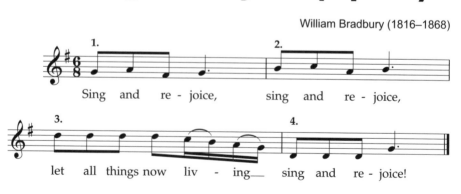

66. The Gum-Drop Bird (4 parts)

Australian Traditional
Arranged BCT

67. I Poor and Well (3 parts)

John Hilton (1599–1657)

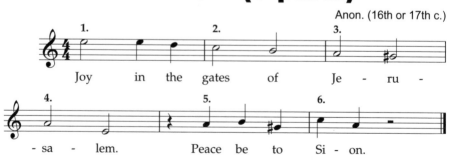

68. The Gates of Jerusalem (6 parts)

Anon. (16th or 17th c.)

69. Frère Jacques (4 parts)

French Traditional
Arranged BCT

70. Sumer is Icumen In (4 parts)

Anon. (13th c.)

Su - mer is i - cum - en in,

Lhu - de sing cuc - cu!

Grow - eth sed and blow - eth med, And

springth the wu - de nu.

Sing Cuc - cu!

Aw - e ble - teth af - ter lomb, Lhouth

71. Gaudeamus hodie! (3 parts)

Anon.

Translation: Let us rejoice today!

72. Why Shouldn't My Goose (4 parts)

Traditional

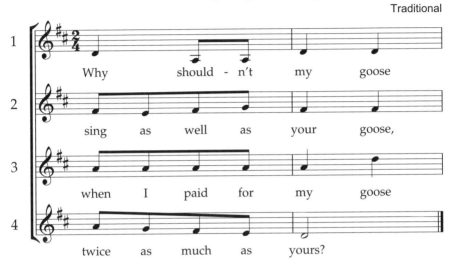

1. Why should - n't my goose

2. sing as well as your goose,

3. when I paid for my goose

4. twice as much as yours?

73. Now the Sky Turns to Red (3 parts)

Barrie Carson Turner

1. Now the sky turns to red, now the sun - light is fad - ing,

2. now the flocks hur - ry home to their safe - ty and shel - ter,

3. eve - ning falls, and the night is be - gin - ning.

74. Three Blind Mice (4 parts)

Traditional
Arranged BCT

75. A Boat, a Boat (3 parts)

John Jenkins (1592–1678)

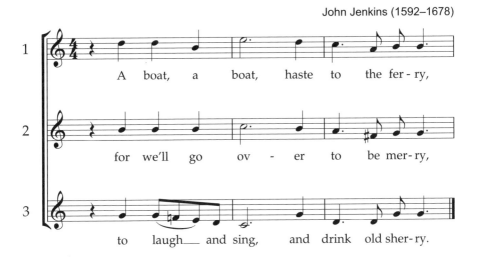

1. A boat, a boat, haste to the fer - ry,
2. for we'll go ov - er to be mer - ry,
3. to laugh__ and sing, and drink old sher - ry.

76. Cuckoo (3 parts)

Edmund Nelham (17th c.)

1. Cuck - oo! Good neigh - bour help us to
2. hedge in the cuck - oo. Keep, keep,
3. keep, oh keep in the cuck - oo.

77. Early to Bed (3 parts)

Traditional
Arranged BCT

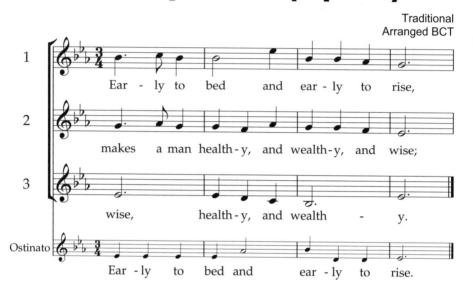

1: Ear - ly to bed and ear - ly to rise,

2: makes a man health-y, and wealth-y, and wise;

3: wise, health-y, and wealth - y.

Ostinato: Ear - ly to bed and ear - ly to rise.

78. White Sand and
Grey Sand (3 parts)

Anon. (18th c.)

1: White sand and grey sand,

2: who'll buy my white sand?

3: Who'll buy my grey sand?

79. Come, Stilly Eventime (3 parts)

Melody: Traditional
Words: BCT

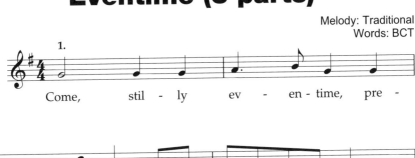

Come, stil - ly ev - en - time, pre -

- pare the way for___ wel - come___ rest.

End - ed, our la - bours, the

glow - ing sun sinks___ in___ the___ west.

Sil - ver, the moon, shin - ing___

down, gild - ing___ all be - low.

80. The Invisible Fox (4 parts)

John Hilton (1599–1657)

1. There was an in-vi-si-ble fox by chance

2. did meet with two vi-si-ble, vi-si-ble geese.

3. He taught them a fine in-vi-si-ble dance

4. for a hun-dred, hun-dred crowns a-piece.

81. Cheese and Bread (4 parts)

Melody: Traditional
Words adapted BCT

1. Cheese and bread!

2. Bread and cheese!

3. Words that go to-geth-er with the

4. great-est ease.

82. Silent Night (3 parts)

Music: Friedrich Silcher (1789–1860)
Original German words: Josef Mohr (1792–1848)
Adapted & arranged BCT

1. Si - lent night! Ho - ly night!
2. round yon vir - gin mo - ther and child,
3. sleep in heav - 'nly peace,_____

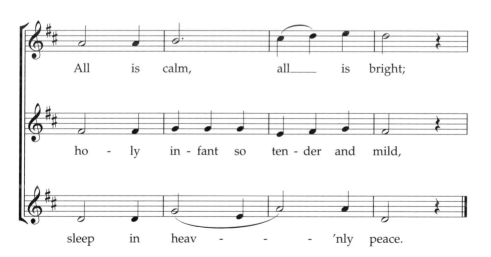

All is calm, all____ is bright;
ho - ly in - fant so ten - der and mild,
sleep in heav - - - 'nly peace.

83. Let the Catch and Toast Go Round (3 parts)

Anon. (18th c.)

84. Hava na shira (3 parts)

Johannes Ockeghem (c.1430–c.1495)
Adapted

Ha - va na shi - ra, shir Al - le - lu - ia.

Ha - va na shi - ra, shir Al - le - lu - ia.

Ha - va na shi - ra, shir Al - le - lu - ia.

Translation: Let us sing, sing *Alleluia*.

85. Hark! The Clock Strikes (4 parts)

Melody: Anon. (19th c.)
Words: BCT

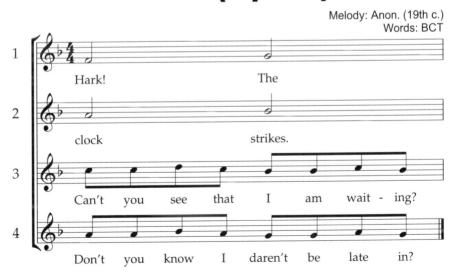

Hark! The

clock strikes.

Can't you see that I am wait - ing?

Don't you know I daren't be late in?

86. London's Burning (4 parts)

Traditional
Arranged BCT

Note: The ostinato singers should stand either side of the choir.

87. Tra-ra, Tra-ra! (4 parts)

Melody: Traditional
Words & Arrangement: BCT

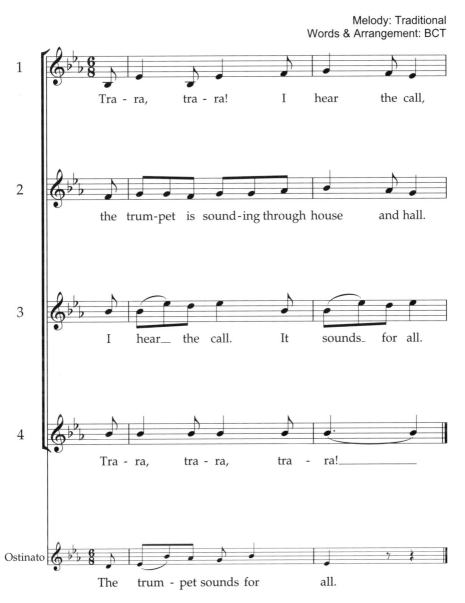

88. Hark! (3 parts)

?William White (c.1585–before1667)

89. Now I Am Married (4 parts)

William Webb (c.1600–after1656)

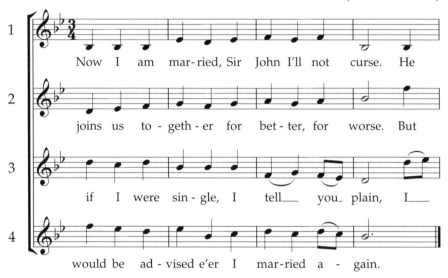

1. Now I am mar-ried, Sir John I'll not curse. He
2. joins us to - geth - er for bet - ter, for worse. But
3. if I were sin - gle, I tell__ you_ plain, I__
4. would be ad - vised e'er I mar - ried a - gain.

90. Alleluia (3 parts)

Franz Schubert (1797–1828)

1. Al - le - lu - ia,
2. al - le - lu - ia, al - - le - lu - ia,
3. al - lel - lu - ia, al - le - lu - ia.

91. The King's Health (3 parts)

Jeremiah Clarke (c.1674–1707)

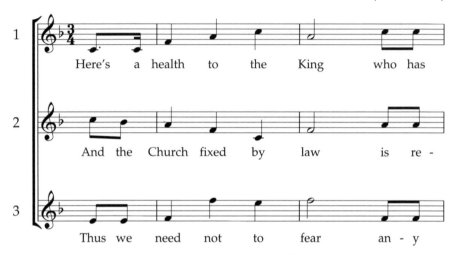

1. Here's a health to the King who has
2. And the Church fixed by law is re -
3. Thus we need not to fear an - y

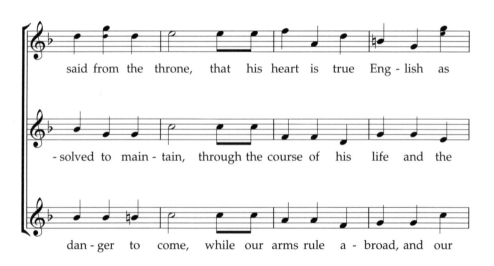

said from the throne, that his heart is true Eng - lish as
- solved to main - tain, through the course of his life and the
dan - ger to come, while our arms rule a - broad, and our

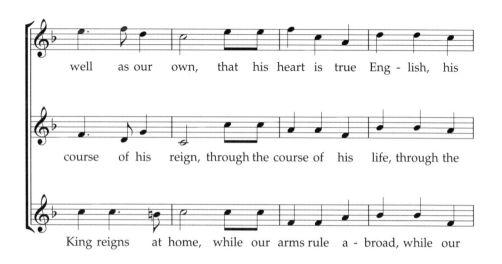

well   as our   own,   that his heart is true Eng - lish, his

course   of his   reign, through the course of his   life, through the

King reigns   at home, while our arms rule a - broad, while our

heart is true Eng - lish as   well   as our   own.

course   of   his   life and the   course   of his   reign.

arms   rule   a - broad and our   King rules   at home.

74

92. Banbury Ale (4 parts)

Anon.

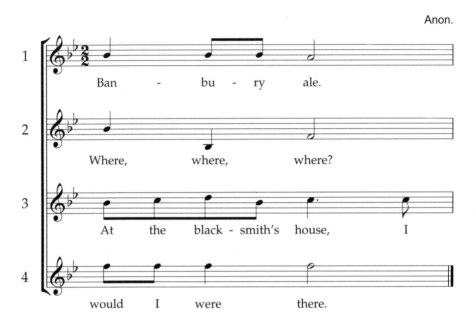

1. Ban - bu - ry ale.

2. Where, where, where?

3. At the black - smith's house, I

4. would I were there.

93. Time for Bed (2 parts)

Melody: Traditional
Words: BCT

1. Time for bed! Time for bed!

2. Time for bed, you sleep - y head!

94. The Mid of the Moon (4 parts)

Anon. (16th or 17th c.)

1. Go to Joan Glo - ver and
2. tell her I love her, and
3. at the mid of the moon
4. I will come to her.

95. The Hart, He Loves the High Wood (4 parts)

Anon. (17th c.)

The hart, he loves the high wood, the hare, he loves the hill. The knight, he loves the bright sword, the la - dy loves her will.

96. The Huntman's Sound (4 parts)

Melody: Traditional
Words: BCT

1. The hunts - man's sound in the green - wood,

2. tra - ra,_____ tra - ra!_____

3. The hunts - man's sound in the win - ter wood,

4. tra - ra,_____ tra - ra!_____

97. Make New Friends, but Keep the Old (4 parts)

Traditional

Make new friends, but keep_ the_ old, for

one is sil - ver and the oth - er gold.

98. Come Hither, Boy (3 parts)

John Hilton (1599–1657)

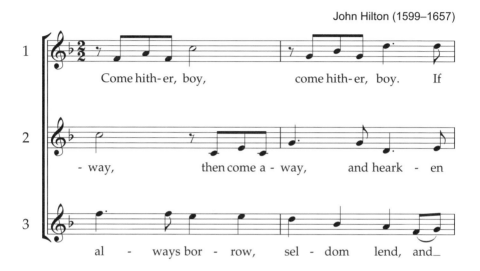

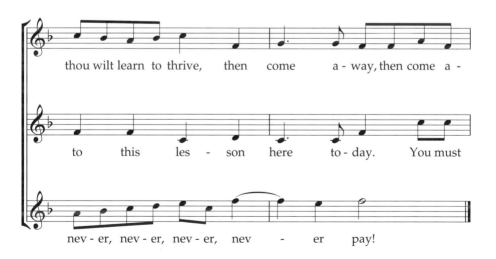

99. Well Rung, Tom (4 parts)

John Miller (17th or 18th c.)

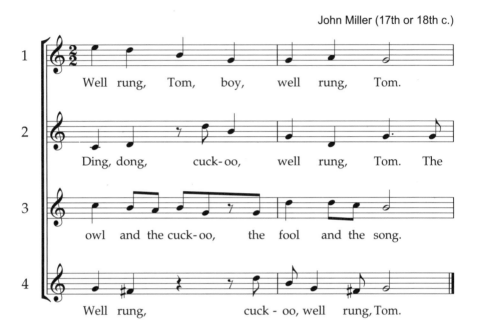

100. Halleluja (2 parts)

Anon.

101. Haste Thee, Nymph (3 parts)

Music: Samuel Arnold (1740–1802)
Words: John Milton (1608–1674)

Haste thee, nymph, and bring with thee,

Jest and youth - ful joli - ty,

Quips and cranks and wan - ton wiles,

Nods and becks and wreath - èd smiles,

Sport that wrink - led care de - rides, And

laugh - ter hold - ing both his sides.

102. So Now, Good Night (4 parts)

Melody: Traditional
Words: BCT

1 Now, good - night! The
2 day is ov - er, eve - ning falls. The
3 sun has set, no black - bird calls, so
4 now, good - night.

103. Angels, Guard Us (4 parts)

Traditional

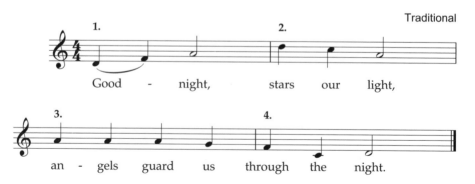

Good - night, stars our light,
an - gels guard us through the night.

104. The Bell Doth Toll (3 parts)

Anon. (19th c.)

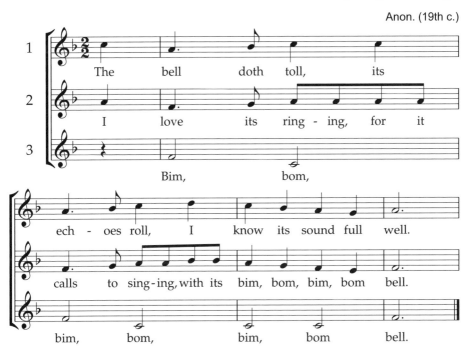

1. The bell doth toll, its ech - oes roll, I know its sound full well.

2. I love its ring - ing, for it calls to sing-ing, with its bim, bom, bim, bom bell.

3. Bim, bom, bim, bom, bim, bom bell.

105. Weavers of the Cloth (3 parts)

Melody: Traditional
Words: BCT

1. Wal - ter weaves the blue cloth,

2. Wes - ley weaves the green cloth,

3. Will - iam weaves the gold cloth.

106. Christmas is Coming (3 parts)

Traditional

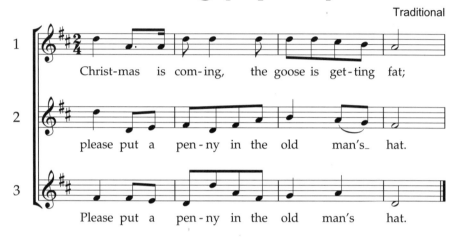

1. Christ-mas is com-ing, the goose is get-ting fat;

2. please put a pen-ny in the old man's_ hat.

3. Please put a pen-ny in the old man's hat.

107. Kiss the Cup (3 parts)

Anon. (17th c.)

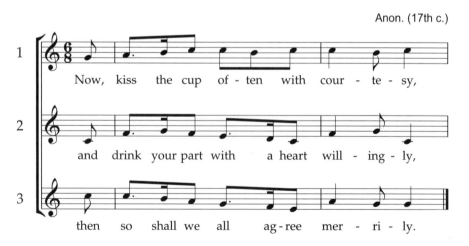

1. Now, kiss the cup of-ten with cour-te-sy,

2. and drink your part with a heart will-ing-ly,

3. then so shall we all ag-ree mer-ri-ly.

          Printed in Germany S&Co.8411

Index by Title

Index by Part